1 MONTH OF
FREE
READING

at
www.ForgottenBooks.com

By purchasing this book you are
eligible for one month membership to
ForgottenBooks.com, giving you
unlimited access to our entire
collection of over 1,000,000 titles via
our web site and mobile apps.

To claim your free month visit:
www.forgottenbooks.com/free922272

ISBN 978-0-260-01372-9
PIBN 10922272

This book is a reproduction of an important historical work. Forgotten Books uses state-of-the-art technology to digitally reconstruct the work, preserving the original format whilst repairing imperfections present in the aged copy. In rare cases, an imperfection in the original, such as a blemish or missing page, may be replicated in our edition. We do, however, repair the vast majority of imperfections successfully; any imperfections that remain are intentionally left to preserve the state of such historical works.

ADDRESS

Delivered before the Ohio Baptist Education Society, at the annual meeting held in Granville, October 6, 1832.—By Elder S. W. Lynd.

In this period of mental resources, and in view of that impulse which has roused up our race from the slumber of ages, the importance and necessity of extensive mental culture are apparent to every reflecting mind. The triumph of the passions over the understanding will be the inevitable result of those principles of freedom, which are so rapidly extending their influence over the nations of the earth, and shaking to their foundation, the long established superstructures of government, unless the cultivation of the intellect be commensurate with the exigency.—When a people begin to understand their political rights, and rise with one heart, to attain freedom or to perish in the attempt, they may succeed in the enterprize. They may declare to the world their independence; but though the sword has achieved the victory, by the sword it cannot be sustained. It requires a moral power based upon the proper improvement of the understanding and the right cultivation of the affections.—This remark may be considered as peculiarly applicable to our own country. Ours is a confederation of several independent States, having in some respects different interests. That local feeling and prejudice, capable of being directed, under the influence of designing men, to civil discord, exist in our land, cannot be concealed. To every thinking man, to every lover of peace and harmony, it is a source of deep regret. These disuniting causes cannot be controlled at the mouth of the cannon or the point of the bayonet. In defence of their civil rights, there is a spirit in the American character that laughs at the spear, and shrinks not from the garment dyed in blood. *"When Greek meets Greek, then comes the tug of war."* Physical force is weakness and madness here. Ours is a social compact, voluntarily entered into for mutual benefit, and if sustained at all, must be voluntarily sustained. All the links of the chain that bind us together are *moral* links—and the diffusion of *moral* power is therefore essential to the preservation of our liberties. But moral power is the result of a cultivated intellect, and sanctified affections. The necessity of extensive mental culture is, consequently, obvious.

But in addition to these considerations, our population is becoming the most varied among the nations. It is the asylum for the oppressed of every land. Men of no education, and men of every degree of education, with all their national habits, and prejudices, are swelling the tide of emigration to this fertile valley.— And when, at no distant day, their votes and those of their children command the decisions of our national counsels, what shall we not have to fear? But should this vast population be subjected to the influence of general education, and virtuous principles, amid all the convulsions of ancient governments, our *Republic*, would stand firm as her towering mountains, around whose summit the storms of heaven have harmlessly played for ages. But the tide is rising and rapidly rolling onward:—whatever is to be done must be done quickly. It is a source of high gratification to the philanthropist, that our countrymen are waking up to the great work. *Mechanics Institutes* and *Lyceums*, in different parts of our land, are imparting knowledge through the medium of public lectures, and instruction in private classes. They are destined to accomplish much in the enlightening of the public mind. The *Press* is supplying daily channels of information, by which the taste for reading is improved, and the mind expanded to all that is *liberal, noble,* and *beneficial*. The common school system, adopted by many States in our Union, is among the best plans, for the general diffusion of knowledge. The Sunday School Institution is also calculated to advance the interests of education, and at the same time to improve the moral feeling. To these may be added, our numerous private Academies of the first order, and the multiplication of colleges for the purpose of liberal education. *Much* is doing, but *much remains* to be done. There is danger in the present state of the world, that some of the most enthusiastic will be satisfied to impart, and their pupils to receive, a range of knowledge exceedingly superficial. This is the present tendency of things, as far as my observation extends. "*A little knowledge is a dangerous thing,*" whenever its possessor is encouraged to believe, that he stands on equal ground with others, whose education has been extensive. It engenders pride, and leads to many unpleasant results. Some knowledge is necessary to all, and a *limited* education of *the many* is preferable to *no* education; but let it be remembered that the child is not the man —neither is the dwarf, the giant. To level intellectual and moral distinction in any land, is to level the very soul of true merit.— In our happy country no man rises in public estimation either by physical superiority, or by the vain *orders* of regal pomp and favor. But there is *one order*, which will always be regarded and always elevate to distinction, in any correct community. It is the *Order* of Intellectual energy. This is the *Order* which a free and well instructed people will elevate to the high seats of our national and State Legislatures, our Judiciaries, our Colleges and our Pulpits. For the common purposes of life, in regard to the general population, a common English education is sufficient, but then let it be distinctly understood by those who obtain it, that it is but a common education. Let them not cherish the fancy that they have acquired all that is sufficient for the purposes of society. If a young man of mental vigor and ambition is determined to break down the barriers that oppose his way to the treasures of knowledge, let him not set out to obtain a *limited* education—but to obtain the most *liberal* that our highest institutions of learning can impart. Let him feel the spirit of Parini, the modern Satiric poet of Dr. Prideaux, who afterwards rose to be Bishop of Worcester. His parents were so poor that they could scarcely keep him at school till he had learned to read and write. He then walked to Oxford and obtained employment in the kitchen of Exeter College, whence he gradually made his way into a fellowship. While I admire the efforts now making to extend to *all* the benefits of education, I cannot but deprecate the opinion entertained by many that the Latin and Greek languages are unnecessary in modern education—and that they present serious obstacles to the acquirement of useful knowledge. It would be easy to show that while a youth is learning these languages, he is acquiring a knowledge of Grammar in general, and a power to analyze his native tongue with ease and efficiency. He is becoming acquainted with important facts and views of other days, and at the same time cultivating a refined taste. He is learning to express his thoughts with correctness and energy.

To read the Poets and the Orators of Greece and Rome in their own language is to hold fellowship with the spirits of those distinguished men—to read them *in a translation*, is to look into their grave and in silent solemnity to gaze upon the *dead*. The form is there, the features are exact, but there is no *life*. Some of the most honored men of modern times, who have enlivened the *world* by the splendor of their imagination, who have infused into multitudes a relish for the more solid acquirements, who have kindled the ardor of nations in the defence of their dearest rights, first imbibed the spirit by which they were animated in the glowing pages of Grecian and Roman literature.

Among the most cheering indications of the rapid growth and prosperity of our country, may be placed the multiplied public Institutions of the first character, where our youth may receive the benefits of a liberal education. It has ceased to be a question among the intelligent whether a public or a private education is to be preferred. In the increasing demand for *able* and *accomplished* teachers, it is apparent that private effort can accomplish a very limited amount of good. At the present day, private teachers of reputation could not be secured to answer half the demand.—The *method*, the *economy*, and the *numbers* which the system of public instruction in colleges embraces, give it a claim to peculiar attention and support. The evils which have been considered as attaching to this system, are increased rather than diminished by private instruction. It is unnatural to suppose that youth are to be confined, by instruction in the family, to the company, the conversation, and the influence of teachers advanced in life. They must have companions like themselves, youthful: they *will* have them. Restraint in this respect, will not only embitter, but destroy the kindest feelings of their nature. Let them be taught right principles, and under the influence of these principles, let them make their choice from their own ranks. If their disposition be vicious, they will find companions after their own heart, in the vicinity of their parent's dwelling, as much as in the crowded halls of a college. They will be liable to greater exposure. In their own neighborhood if they associate at all, they must associate with youth, who are under no uniform mode of instruction, influenced by the example of parents of all descriptions and varied in their principles, restrained by different plans of discipline or suffered to act their own pleasure, without the corrective of a wholesome government. In Colleges they select their companions from those who are passing through the same course of education, the same discipline, and who are under the influence of the same moral principles, as far as the effort of their instructors can accomplish this desirable object.

Our country can boast Institutions of learning of a rival character to those of Europe. Our *Harvard*, our *Yale*, our *Nassau Hall*, and others that might be named, are distinguished on the roll of classical fame. And in this far-off West where but yesterday the first strokes of the Pioneer's axe, resounded through the forest—and where villages, and towns, and cities have arisen as by magic—we can glory in the fact, that *we too* have colleges which would do honor to any clime, and which are destined to place our sons among the most favored of the earth in relation to science.

The association of physical and mental education may be regarded as a new era in the history of literature and science. It combines economy with utility, and places a liberal education within the power of the poorest. It unites strength of constitution with vigor of intellect, and removes the apprehensions of the parental bosom with respect to the fatal influence of severe study upon the health.

This association of physical and mental education is contemplated in the design of the Institution whose interests have collected us together this day.

With the afflictive dispensation, which has thus far frustrated the execution of this design you are probably familiar. The buildings which were erected on the farm in the vicinity of this place for the accommodation of young men, pupils of the Institution, were, in May last, when nearly completed, consumed by fire. The friends of the Institution are prepared in holy confidence to employ the language of the Apostle Paul, *"cast down, but not destroyed."* They hope in God that other buildings, now in preparation will rise to his glory. The principal and professors are men decidedly qualified for the business of instruction, and enthusiastic in their respective departments. Here our young men may receive a solid education, and avail themselves of advantages not inferior to those presented by any college in the West.

As soon as the contemplated buildings are finished, the pupils will be removed to the farm, and the benefits of the *manual* education system will, we hope, be manifest to all.

I have said that *moral* power is the result of a cultivated intellect and sanctified affections. The latter embraces all true morality and virtue in the divine estimation. The intellect may be improved in various branches of science, and yet the heart be depraved; and hence the idea entertained by some that knowledge and virtue are convertible terms, is not only absurd, but at once destroys all moral obligation, for if the absence of virtue is the absence of knowledge, or, in other words, if the want of virtue is attributable to ignorance, and not to design, there can be no criminality.— Education is communicating an impulse to society that will be found either beneficial or injurious, according to the direction which it may receive. We have done but little towards the virtue and the happiness of our race, when we have erected colleges, and given to our children a liberal education. Sciences are useful, arts are useful, but the knowledge of ourselves, of our duty to God, and supreme love of him, are the finishing of our education.

The great medium of imparting religious instruction, and sanctifying the affections, is, by the determination of heaven, *the preaching of the gospel.* Sunday Schools, Tract Societies, and Bible Societies, are valuable institutions, but when the pulpit is frequently made a place of exhibiting their value, and an instrument of collecting money for their support, instead of preaching Christ to sinners, it is *the pulpit degraded.* Let it never be forgotten, that the preaching of the gospel, is the *appointed* instrumentality for the conversion of the world; that it has, in all ages, received the *sanction of divine blessing;* and that it is decidedly the *most effi-*

cient instrumentality in the advance of evangelical truth. : By this means, the strong holds of satan are prostrated and glory results to God. With the impulse which general education is now communicating to society, the progress of evangelical means should be commensurate, and among these, as a prominent measure, the proclamation of the gospel, by qualified men.

The society, it is my happiness to address this day, contemplates the instruction of young men for the ministry. They disavow any design of *making* ministers, or, of preparing persons by education to preach, whom God has not called to the work. All they *can do*, and all they *expect* to do, is to assist young men who have been approved by churches and licensed, with such information on various topics, as may contribute to their future usefulness in the world.

The apprehension which some of our brethren entertain that education will make our ministers proud and vain-glorious, is altogether a mistake. Men of limited information are more liable to be exalted in their own estimation, than those are who have been permitted to ascend the hill of science. The latter discover how little of all the vast field before them is occupied, and their spirits are humbled. But will Zion be disgraced by knowledge? by her ministers being well informed men?

A young man who believes that he is called to preach the gospel, and who, upon his entrance into the ministry is flattered into the belief that he possesses extraordinary talents, very naturally concludes that he is superior to all others. He grows *vain, proud,* and *overbearing*. He is too great to be taught, and never fails to prove himself a weak man whenever he rises to preach. But let him be sent to a Theological Institution, and mingle for a few years, with those who have the same object in view. He will find competitors—he will come into contact with those who know full as much as he does, and frequently more. He will be disappointed in his calculations of his own greatness. After measuring his powers a few times with his class-mates, he will learn to descend a little from the pinnacle of his fancied superiority. This, of necessity, will lead to humility, and induce him through life not to think more highly of himself than he ought to think.

Several important principles are to be recognized in regard to the ministerial office.

1. In order to a faithful discharge of the duties of their office, ministers must be sincere and humble followers of Christ. They must deny themselves, take up their cross, and submit to the holy government of their Lord. They must have an experimental acquaintance with the son of God. As it is their duty to preach the depravity of the human heart, they must know, by experience,

its depravity,'or they cannot teach others; neither can they comfort them when burdened with sin. Since it is theirs to call men to repentance, they must first have repented themselves, otherwise they cannot describe this exercise, and of course they will be but blind leaders of the blind. Engaged to direct men to the Lamb of God, by faith, they must know what it is to believe, they must feel the efficacy of his blood in their own hearts. In other words, to be a christian minister, a man must be a christian himself.

2. Ministers of the gospel must have a call to this work. "No man taketh this honor to himself but he that is called of God, as was Aaron." Two things enter into this call. The first is a deep and abiding sense of necessity. The apostle Paul says, "Necessity is laid upon me, and woe unto me, if I preach not the gospel." The other requisite is, that the person who thinks himself the subject of a divine call, have suitable natural abilities for this work. These can usually be discovered by a church, if she is careful to mark the gifts of those who form a part of her number. Sometimes they are discovered in an individual before he himself is willing to suppose that he possesses them. It is the duty of every church when any of her members exhibit suitable talents for this great work, to direct their attention to the subject, to encourage them to exercise their gifts, and to urge upon them the solemn consideration, whether it is not their duty to be thus engaged.

3. Ministers of the gospel must be persons who are qualified for their office by a suitable education in divine subjects. No men were more eminently prepared for their station in this respect, than the disciples of our Lord. They were possessed of good natural powers. They attended the instructions of Christ himself for about three years. They had many opportunities of receiving explanations, upon subjects which they did not comprehend. The customs and manners of the East which are so extensively referred to in the sacred writings, and the understanding of which is absolutely essential to the elucidation of many of the most interesting and useful portions of the sacred word—the Geography of the country, which is spread through all parts of the Bible—the climate, soil, productions and animals of those regions which are frequently adopted in illustration, or referred to incidentally—the parables and proverbs which were common among the orientals, and upon which Christ founded some of his most valuable remarks —all these were in some measure familiar to the disciples of our Lord. But we have to learn them, and, at this distance of time, with considerable labor, in order to enter into the spirit and beauty of the inspired records.

From the day of Pentecost, the apostles were under a special divine influence.—They had the power of working miracles in confirmation of their mission, and they could speak in different languages, all of which they received as a gift without the aid of study. But at the present day we have to acquire a knowledge of languages by hard labor of thought and memory, either under the tuition of others, or by our own diligence. Some professors of religion estimate a minister in proportion to his ignorance, and if he spend as long a period in a Theological School, as Christ's disciples spent under his tuition, they fancy him unfit for the ministerial office. I have known men who never had the advantage which a Theological Institution affords, who were eminently useful in the kingdom of Christ. The labors of such men will be held in remembrance. There were two traits of importance, however, in these men, that rendered them worthy of the affections of all God's children. In the first place, they never ceased to regret the want of a suitable education; and, in the second place, they were unremitting, as far as their means would justify, to supply this deficiency by self-instruction. They were men of industry, of investigating minds, and endeavored to prepare themselves, by an ardent study of the sacred volume, with such collateral helps as they could procure, for the exhibition of plain and practical truths. But they labored under serious disadvantages, which they could not but feel through life. Some of the first men as to intellectual culture, that ever occupied the sacred desk, rose, under the blessing of God, by their own labors; yet even with respect to them, *it was all up hill.* The means of suitable instruction would greatly have assisted them in their ascent to knowledge. These are the men who advocate Colleges and Theological Schools.

That a man may be a useful and successful minister of the gospel without a knowledge of the language in which it was written, is not doubted; but it does not follow from this fact, that such a knowledge is not desirable. It is exceedingly desirable. It is a satisfaction to a minister himself not to be dependant upon others for a translation of the sacred volume.

If a man will not avail himself of instruction when it is offered to him, nor make any attempt to instruct himself in sacred subjects, and in others that may contribute to his understanding of the Bible—if he is so idle, that, having obtained one particular range of thought, he dwells on it while life continues, the probability is that he will accomplish but little good, and bring but little credit to the cause of Christ. At the present day, education, to the minister of the gospel, is peculiarly necessary. He is bound to advocate a system that is dearer to him than life, and he desires the best kind of weapons. Men must be reasoned with, if we would do them any good. Infidelity is now supported by men whose education enables them to triumph over the ignorant; and the evidences of the truth of our holy religion ought therefore to be understood. Men of learning contest the correctness of our present translation of the Bible, in order to support false doctrines; they introduce history, geography, and oriental customs, and apply them to their own purpose; they influence the minds of serious enquirers; and when these perplexed individuals turn to the ministers of the altar to have their anxieties removed, they may be told by these defenders of the truth, we know nothing about those things; we have never studied them; we have no books to inform us, if we wished to know. Hence the importance of education. No man in the ministry, even in advanced life, ought to rest satisfied with his present attainments. It is not *age*, but *indolence*, that keeps back from the acquirement of knowledge. Every minister ought to be willing to study his defects, to receive the advice of his brethren in relation to them, and to improve, were he as advanced in life as Methuselah. One of the most prominent defects in preaching is that habit which some have of introducing all the doctrines of the gospel into one sermon, let the text be what it may. It suits an idle man who considers study a weariness too great to be endured—but what is study? It is *thought*. It suits one therefore who has not sufficient energy *to think.* It may sound well to preach a summary of the whole gospel at once—but as this kind of preaching costs no *thought*, and but little *practice*—it will not lead the hearers to *think.* But an ignorant man is obliged to pursue this course, or to give up his ministerial office. The mind never acts with power but when it has one single subject before it for contemplation. Every thing that is read or studied with a view to illustrate this particular subject, affords interest both to the speaker and the hearer. But a mind of this character will seek knowledge with undeviating intensity nor tire in the glorious pursuit, and the possesser of such a mind ceases to be an ignorant man.

The object of Theological education is, not, that our ministers may hold the pen of controversy, but that they may be prepared for their duties in the pulpit. Zeal is of vast importance in the ministry, but zeal without knowledge is a disgrace to those who are called *Elders* in the church. The opposer of religion enters the field of deep investigation, travels the mazes of criticism, and if the minister of the gospel cannot meet him, he betrays the sacred cause, which he has come forth professedly to defend. It is not by meeting an infidel or a heretic publicly, and entering into a debate of three or four days, that much good is accomplished; but by exhibiting the truth from the pulpit, *consistently* and *forcibly.* To show the harmony of any passage, we attempt to illustrate, with matter of fact, and to exhibit sound principles of interpretation; will do more to sweep away incorrect conceptions aud strong, objections from the mind of the hearer, than can be effected by a public controversy. But to illustrate the word of God in this manner requires considerable knowledge,

The principle is a correct one that the minister of the gospel should not be inferior to his hearers in that kind of knowledge which is necessary for the clear and consistent developement of divine truth. The time has been when a limited degree of education, with deep piety was sufficient to the general purposes of religious instruction—but in this land, even in this far-off West, that time has passed, or is now rapidly passing away. The march of mind is *onward*. Education is becoming general, and a liberal education too is possessed by many in all parts of this valley.— Even the Sunday School children are greatly in advance of their fathers, and I may add, in some instances, in advance of ministers of the gospel, in respect to biblical knowledge.

The time has come, when Theological Institutions should cease to be regarded with a jealous eye, by those who desire the prosperity of Zion. The numerous presses established in our land, by which information may be communicated to the people—the general effort to have all our youthful population, able to read— and the religious liberty which all are permitted to enjoy, are among the facilities for establishing the kingdom of Christ in the earth; but then let it be remembered, that these are facilities also for the prince of darkness to extend his kingdom. If there are *presses* for the dissemination of divine truth, the same means may be employed to spread abroad infidel and heretical opinions. If children generally are taught to read, they may read publications of a *corrupting*, as well as those of a *virtuous* tendency. If religious liberty is the privilege of all, Satan may induce, and does induce multitudes to make it the occasion of licentiousness. If liberal education enables the advocate of Christianity to maintain his ground in these perilous times, it also furnishes the vicious mind with the most efficient weapons against the truth. It is sometimes said in opposition to the benevolent efforts of the day—"*We did very well before religious Newspapers, and other publications were sent forth among us, when we had scarcely any book to read but our Bibles: We did very well before Theological Institutions were advocated among us, or Sunday Schools, Missionary Societies, and Bible Societies were organized.*" But here is the appropriate answer. The facilities which I just stated, were capable of being employed to the establishment of Satan's kingdom, and this must have been their influence in the hands of worldly men. This will be their influence still, unless christians employ them, and occupy the whole ground of moral culture, with greater

energy than ever. The church of God has not created the cir-
cumstances in which she is placed. The providence of the Almighty has surrounded her with a population thirsting for knowledge, and determined to have knowledge of some kind or other.
The human mind is on the advance. Its accumulating resources
cannot be arrested. Error and misery will overwhelm the earth,
unless christians under the guidance of the Holy Spirit, can give
a proper direction to these resources. Shall the facilities of education which the present times furnish, be employed to strengthen
infidelity, to give popularity to error, and to sink into the lowest
estimation in society, the instructers in evangelical truth? And
when the providence of God directly intimates the necessity of
education in the ministry, and places within the reach of all, the
means for its acquirement, shall we be found fighting against God?

The number of young men, in our denomination, in this state
alone, who have been called to the work of the ministry, by the
churches, is considerable; and it is a source of pleasure that they
possess good native powers, which under proper culture would
make them extensively useful. Why should they not receive the
advantages of education? Why should they not, for a time be train-
ed to regular and severe thinking? Why should they not acquire
the command of language to communicate their thoughts intelli-
gibly to others? Why should they not be qualified to exercise an
influence in society? The immediate necessity of their labors
ought not to be pleaded,—because the usefulness of a man's life
is not estimated by detail, but by the aggregate. In the present
advancing state of society, the usefulness of an ignorant young
man is in an inverse ratio to his increase in years. Of this fact,
experience is the proof, and many will feel its force at sixty, who
ridicule education at thirty. Let our young men beware how they
slight the acquirement of knowledge. They will discover their
error before many years, when no claims to inspiration will shield
them from neglect.

Far be it from me to cast the least reflection upon those pious
men, who were the pioneers of the Saviour in this western country. They have done nobly. They were suited to the times, and
this fact will always command for them respect. Their whitened
locks proclaim that they are men of other days, and seal the lips
of our youth in awe. When we listen to them, we listen to the
voice of venerable age, of experience, and of faith. We forget
that they are uneducated men. They were specially adapted by
providence to those times which tried men's souls. Yet these, our
fathers in the ministry, if they were now about to commence their
course, would esteem it a favor to have some preparatory education in a Theological school, suited to the present advanced state

of society. Were they now addressing our young brethren on
the subject I know they would say, "Brethren, avail yourselves of
every honorable means to obtain a preparatory education—you will
have occasion for all the knowledge you can command in these
days of infidelity and heresy. Lay in a good stock for the time
to come, for when you are once in the field your opportunities for
study will be greatly abridged." But the work of these aged fathers, is about to terminate. Their counsel and example will soon
be removed from among us. *God Almighty*, bless them, crown
their evening of life with peace, and raise up many faithful laborers
in the vineyard when their heads shall be laid low with the clods of
the valley.

ANNUAL MEETING OF THE OHIO BAPTIST EDUCATION SOCIETY.

The Society met in Granville, Saturday October 6th, 1832.—
At 11 o'clock, according to previous appointment, an appropriate
address was delivered before the society by Elder S. W. Lynd, of
Cincinnati. [See the address on the preceding pages.] The
society was then called to order, Elder Lynd one of the Vice
Presidents having taken the chair.

The following members were present and handed in their annu-
al contributions of one dollar each, viz. Allen Darrow, John Ste-
vens, Charles Sawyer, S. Spelman, Wm. Sedwick, J. Pratt, James
Berry, Paschal Carter, Jacob Drake, Alanson Sinnet, Leonard B.
Woods, Jon. Atwood, Ephraim Emerson, Evan Crane, Daniel
Shepardson, Andrew Hyde, Jesse Frey, W. M. Wilson, A. H.
Frink.

On motion, resolved that a committee of three be appointed to
nominate six trustees for the Granville Literary and Theological
Institution; and that Allen Darrow, John Stevens and John Mc-
Leod be this committee.

On motion, resolved that a committee of three be appointed to
nominate officers of the Education Society for the ensuing year;
and that Wm. Sedwick, Charles Sawyer, and Jacob Drake be this
committee.

Adjourned to half past 2 o'clock. Elder Drake prayed.

HALF PAST 2 O'CLOCK, P. M.—Society met according to ad-
journment. Prayer by brother L. B. Woods.

The Committee for nominating six trustees of the Institution,
reported the following names:—Lucius D. Mower, John Pratt,
S. W. Lynd, John McLeod, Charles Sawyer, Wm. S. Richards.

On motion, resolved that the report of the committee be accepted, and that the persons named therein be appointed Trustees of
the Granville Literary and Theological Institution.

The committee for nominating officers of the Education Society being called upon, reported as follows:—Jacob Drake, *President;* —Francis Dunlavy, Geo. C. Sedwick, Wm. Sutton, Geo. Jeffries, John Prichard, N. Cory, Edward Welsh, James Lyon, J. Baily, Wm. Wall, *Vice Presidents;*—Allen Darrow, *Secretary;*—Chas. Sawyer, *Treasurer;*—Samuel Carpenter, Wm. Sedwick, William Spencer, James Berry, —————————, Geo. Jeffries, G. M. Peters, *Directors.* The report of the committee was accepted, and choice was made accordingly.

The Trustees of the Institution, according to a requisition of the 5th article of the Constitution of the Education Society, presented through their Secretary, a report of their proceedings, &c. during the past year. [See the report below.]

The report was accepted.

After hearing the report of the Trustees of the Institution, which gave, in most respects, a very gratifying view of its progress, and its prospects, the two following resolutions were passed:—

1. *Resolved,* That the measures which have been pursued by the Trustees for advancing the interests of the Institution, meet our cordial approbation: and especially that, in our view, the debt which has been accumulated for building purposes could not have been avoided.

2. *Resolved,* That after deducting the loss by fire, the farm and buildings belonging to the Institution, seem to us a fair equivalent for the expenditures which have been made; and that to relieve the Institution of the debt which has been thus necessarily incurred, we individually pledge our strenuous exertions.

On motion, resolved that the thanks of this Society be presented to Elder S. W. Lynd for the address delivered by him on this occasion, and that a copy be requested for publication.

On motion, resolved that the publishers of the Newark Gazette, Republican Advocate, and of the Ohio State Journal, and the publishers of other papers in this State friendly to the cause of education, be requested to publish the report of the Trustees of the Institution.

On motion, resolved that the executive committee of the Trustees of the Institution be requested to appoint a suitable person to deliver an address at the next annual meeting of the Society, and to give seasonable notice of such appointment.

On motion, resolved that the 6th article of the constitution of this Society be so altered and amended that the annual meeting be held on Thursday following the second Wednesday in August.

On motion, adjourned to meet in Granville at the time appointed for the next annual meeting.

Prayer by Elder J. Berry.   S. W. LYND, *Vice President.*
   A. DARROW, Sec.

CONSTITUTION AS AMENDED.

Art. 1. This Society shall be called *The Regular Baptist Education Society* of Ohio.

Art. 2. The object of this Society shall be to promote sound Literature and Science, including the Literary and Theological improvement of pious young men for the ministry.

Art. 3. This Society shall consist of delegates from Regular Baptist Churches, and Education Societies auxiliary to this, in the ratio of two delegates to every $5 paid annually, and of such individuals as shall pay one dollar annually; and any person paying at one time twenty dollars, shall be a member for life.

Art. 4. The officers of this Society shall consist of a President and as many Vice Presidents as they shall choose from time to time to elect, a Secretary and Treasurer, who with seven others shall constitute a Board of Directors, any five of whom shall constitute a quorum, and *all of whom shall be members in good standing in Regular Baptist Churches.* The duties of the President, Secretary and Treasurer, shall be the same as they are in other similar societies. It shall be the duty of the Board of Directors generally to superintend the interests of the Society, and particularly to examine applicants for the patronage of the Society, and determine the time and place and course of their studies. The Board shall make their own by-laws, and regulate their own meetings, and make a detailed report of their proceedings annually to the Society.

Art. 5. The Society shall have power to establish one or more Literary or Theological Seminaries, and to appoint Trustees for the government of the same, which number thus appointed, shall not be less than twelve, nor more than thirty-six, to be chosen for three years, one third of whom shall be elected annually, who shall appoint their own officers, make their own by-laws, and report to the Society at their annual meeting, to whom they are held responsible for their proceedings.

Art. 6. This Society shall meet annually on Thursday following the second Wednesday in August, at such place as the Society shall annually determine, at which time the officers and Directors of the Society shall be chosen by ballot.

Art. 7. This constitution may be altered at any annual meeting, by a vote of two-thirds of the members present; so much of the 4th Article to be inviolate as relates to the church membership of the officers and Directors of this Society.

ANNUAL MEETING OF THE 'TRUSTEES OF THE GRANVILLE LIT-
ERARY AND THEOLOGICAL INSTITUTION.—*Granville, October 6th,*
1832.

[The principal doings of the Trustees follow.]
Previous to the meeting of the Education Society, the Trustees
met, heard and. adopted the report which had been prepared re-
specting the affairs of the Institution, and directed their Secretary
to present the same to the Education Society.   [See report below.]

Saturday evening, 7 o'clock.. The committee appointed at the
last annual meeting, to obtain an act of incorporation of the Institution; reported that they had attended to the duty assigned
them, which report was accepted.

John McLeod, Geo. Jeffries, and Wm. S. Richards were appointed a committee to procure an amendment to the act of incorporation, if found necessary.

S. W. Lynd, John Pratt, and Geo. C. Sedwick were appointed
a committee to procure by donation, philosophical apparatus for
the Institution.

On motion, it was resolved to appoint an executive committee
of seven, to transact the business of the Institution the ensuing
year, and that four of said committee be a quorum; and that they
report to the board at their next annual meeting, or sooner if re-
quired.

On motion, resolved that John Stevens and Prof. Pratt be a
committee to nominate officers of the board, including the executive committee.

The committee of nomination made report as follows:—
John McLeod, *President;*—Allen Darrow, *Secretary;*—Paschal
Carter, *Treasurer;*—Sylvester Spelman, Daniel Shepardscn, Chas.
Sawyer, John Pratt, Allen Darrow, L. D. Mower, Jon. Atwood,
Executive Committee.

On motion, resolved that the report be accepted and the persons
named be appointed to the offices specified.

Monday morning, October 8th. [The subject of appointing
agents to solicit funds for the relief of the Institution was referred
to the executive committee.]

On motion, resolved that the executive committee be instructed
to procure as full an attendance as possible at the next annual
meeting of the Education Society.

On motion, resolved that a committee of three consisting of
S. W. Lynd, J. Stevens and J. Pratt, be appointed to prepare and
cause to be published the proceedings of the Education Society
and of the Trustees, including Mr. Lynd's address, and including
also a Circular Addresss to the public.

C

Annual Report of the Trustees of the Granville Literary and Theological Institution, October 6th, 1832.

In accordance with their Constitutional duty, the Trustees of the Granville Literary and Theological Institution exhibit, to the Ohio Baptist Education Society, the sum of their proceedings during the past year, together with the character and the present condition and wants of the Institution under their care, in the following

REPORT.

State of Affairs at the last Annual Meeting.—It will be recollected, that, previous to the last annual meeting, purchase had been made, for the use of the Institution, of a large farm, situated about one mile distant from the town of Granville. It was occupied by a commodious brick mansion-house partly unfinished. The necessary additions and repairs to the house had been commenced; and choice had been made of a Principal to take charge of the Institution.

Professors and Department of Instruction.—Agreeably to the expectation expressed at our last annual meeting, ELDER JOHN PRATT accepted his appointment as Principal of the Institution, and having arrived in Granville, entered upon the discharge of his duties early in December last, at which time the Institution commenced its operations. Mr. PASCHAL CARTER, having been previously appointed an additional Professor, commenced his services in June last, at the beginning of the third term. Mr. ALEXANDER H. FRINK has been employed as an assistant Teacher, from the commencement of the second Term.

The average number of students, during the first quarter, was about thirty; and during the two succeding quarters was upwards of sixty. The number remains about the same the present (fourth) quarter, the want of accommodations prevents their increase. It is confidently expected that the spacious edifice, now in progress of erection on the Institution farm, will be completed by the first of December next. Ample accommodations will then be in readiness for those who are now waiting to become members of the Institution. A very large majority of the present number of students design to prosecute their studies through an extended course of education.

The exercises of the Institution have as yet been carried on in the town of Granville, and will be continued here till the completion of the new edifice on the farm. Its progress, so far as it has depended on the number and character of the students, and on the qualifications and assiduity of the instructers, has been most highly satisfactory. The quarterly examinations have been witnessed by some of the Board, and have evinced, in a very pleasing degree,

(19)

aptness to learn and diligence on the part of the pupils, and aptness to teach, and an enthusiastic ardor in their pursuit on the par-
of instructers.

Buildings.—Owing to the early and severe setting in of the last
winter, the additions and repairs of the buildings for the Institution
were not completed during the previous autumn: and just as
they were nearly finished, in the early part of May last, they
were entirely destroyed by fire. This was indeed a heavy ca-
lamity; and it has been severely felt. It has retarded our progress; but it has not caused us to relax our efforts. It spread a
temporary gloom over the prospects of our rising Institution; but
we believe it will ere long occasion the sun of its prosperity to
shine with the brighter lustre. Measures were very soon taken for
the erection, on the site of the destroyed building, of a new edifice,
which is now rapidly going forward. We expect to see it ready to
be occupied early in December. When completed, it will answer
the purposes of the Institution far better than the former building.
It is pleasantly situated on the Columbus road, presenting a front
towards the south of 82 feet, and being 30 feet wide. A wing of
44 feet by 20 extends back from the main building, so as with it to
present a west front of 74 feet. The whole edifice is three stories
nigh, besides the basement; and is judiciously divided into apart-
ments for the accommodation of the Steward's family, the Professors, for study rooms, dormitories, recitation rooms, &c.

Financial concerns.—The accounts for the first building not
being entirely settled up, and the new building being still in progress, it is impracticable at present to give a perfect statement
throughout of the financial affairs of the Institution. The following, however, we believe to be substantially correct.

The sum of $3400 was contracted to be paid for the farm be-
longing to the Institution, and this sum was raised by subscription for the benefit of the Institution, with the view of being applied to this purpose. This subscription has not as yet been all
paid in; but with a very trifling exception, it is supposed that it
will all be realized.

The additions and repairs of the first building, which was burnt,
were made at an expence of about $2300. The subscriptions for
the farm were partly applied, by a vote of the Trustees at their last
annual meeting, to meet the expense of these additions and repairs; so that the debt contracted for the farm, and for the building which was burnt, and which is still unprovided for, amounts to
not far from the last named sum, viz. $2300.

The value of the mansion-house on the farm at the time of purchase, estimated at $1200, added to the cost of the additions and
repairs, makes our loss by fire $3500.

The expense of the new building cannot now be determined accurately. Including the necessary furniture, it will probably be from five to six thousand dollars,—say about $5500. To meet this expense something like $2800 have been raised by subscripsion, leaving about $2700 to be provided for this purpose. This sum added to the debt of $2300 for the farm and first building, together with unforeseen contingencies, will constitute a debt, when the new edifice is completed, of something more than $5000. To raise this sum will require our vigorous exertions, and the prompt and cheerful co-operation of a generous public.

General Object and Plan.—Our object has been, and is, to build up a useful Institution—suited to the wants, and calculated to promote the welfare of a rapidly growing and free country, where virtuous intelligence, industry and enterprise are sure to meet a quick reward. It designs to embrace, agreeably to its appellation, two departments, Literary and Theological. In the literary department, we aim to establish such a course of instruction as will fit the youth of our country to be skilful instructers of our common schools, and for the ready and accurate transaction of business; whether in public or private life. It is our purpose to furnish the means of obtaining a thorough classical and English education, which shall not be inferior to what can be obtained in any institution, of whatever name, in the western country. The Theological department is designed specially for those young men, members of the Baptist denomination, whom their respective churches judge to be called to the ministry. This description of students will enjoy all the advantages of the Literary department; and in addition to these advantages, will have their attention directed to such studies and exercises as will serve to render their labours in their appropriate work more efficient and acceptable than otherwise they would be.

The large and excellent farm attached to the Institution, will not only be of essential utility to the boarding establishment, but will greatly facilitate the prosecution of the manual labor system, on the part of the students. It is our purpose to make such arrangements that those young men, who feel disposed, may spend a part of each day in profitable manual labor, which, without at all interfering with their progress in study, will serve the double purpose of preserving health and sustaining in part their current expenses.

Conclusion.—We thus present to the Education Society, and through this medium to the public, a concise statement of the affairs of our Institution. They are such as to afford us strong grounds of encouragement. The Institution is furnished with instructers of tried skill and competency; its catalogue of students shows in this respect an ample share of patronge; it has received, and is still receiving the generous contributions of the community in the midst of which it is placed. We have experienced a heavy loss by fire; but this loss can be retrieved. There are now needed our own exertions to complete the arrangements already commenced, and the pecuniary aid of the friends of education, to enable us to clear off the debt of the Institution. Our own strenuous exertions we pledge; for the generous and prompt contributions of our friends, we confidently hope. With these exertions and with this aid, if a benignant Providence smile upon our undertaking, we may anticipate success.

CIRCULAR ADDRESS.

Prepared by the committee appointed for the purpose, in behalf of the Granville Literary and Theological Institution.

The Board of Trustees appointed by the Baptist Education Society of the State of Ohio, having under their charge the interests of the Granville Literary and Theological Institution, would express their gratitude to Almighty God for his favors during the past year. They have been permitted to witness the commencement of an Institution, which promises, under the divine blessing, to equal in usefulness any similar establishment in this great Valley of the West.

A considerable number of young men are already receiving the advantages which its course of instruction embraces, and many more are waiting the completion of suitable buildings upon the farm, for their accommodation.

The Professors are men whose talents and devotedness to the cause of learning, would confer honor on any Institution, and render its literary and scientific facilities, highly efficient. The Board cannot but lament the heavy loss which has been sustained by the burning of their buildings in May last. We hope, however, that its friends will be induced from its misfortunes, as well as from its importance to the denomination, to cherish it with greater ardor than ever. Indeed, we confidently entertain the opinion, that God, in his merciful providence, has permitted this affliction, with a view to the increase of its patrons. Should this prove to be the result, we shall have occasion to rejoice.

It will be perceived from the annual report, that a considerable sum will be necessary to relieve the Institution from its embarrassments. It was not the design of the officiating board in Granville to involve themselves in debt. Yet this they have done, and done as matter of necessity. They labored under a heavy responsibility. Professors were on the spot, and engaged in their duties—a number of pupils had commenced their course—the farm was lying idle. One of two plans was necessary,—either to abandon the undertaking for the present, dismiss pupils and teachers, and, in all probability, render the establishment of a similar Institution among the Baptists almost impossible for years to come—or to assume the responsibility of erecting new buildings upon the most economical plan, and rely upon the faith of the denomination to sustain them in the effort. After much anxiety of mind upon the subject, they finally agreed to adopt the latter. A large frame edifice, is now in progress, calculated for the accommodation of a large number of students.

The members of the Education Society at their late annual meeting, visited the premises and expressed their high satisfaction with the arrangements of the buildings, and the operations of the Board of Trustees.

Greater efforts than have yet been made will be necessary to relieve the Institution from its embarrassments. We would appeal to the friends of education generally in our State, and urge the consideration, that whatever means contribute to elevate the standard of learning among us, will be ultimately a benefit and an honor to the State itself. We wish it to be distinctly understood, that as far as this Institution is *literary*, it is open and free to all, and attempts to exert no influence whatever in the religious tenets of those who may avail themselves of its advantages. On the other hand, as far as its character is *Theological*, the views of our own denomination will be impressed upon those who have been called by the churches to officiate in the ministry.

While therefore, as an Institution designed to promote the cause of literature and science, we feel a liberty in soliciting aid from the friends of education generally—yet to *Baptists principally* we appeal, as its originators. We presume it is not a question among us, whether such an Institution is desirable or not. If any think it is not, we can expect no aid from them. But to those who believe that it will be valuable to the denomination—we ask—"*Is it worth the sacrifice of near* 6000 *dollars?*" That this is but a small sacrifice compared with the advantages that will result from its offering, appears scarcely to admit of a doubt. Shall we then abandon it, or shall we come nobly to the work and sustain it? Abandon it! Let not the thought have a place in our minds for a single moment. Brethren, we must look forward, consider the advancing state of our country, and then, if we are willing as a people to fall in the rear of all others, within a few years from the present time, let us abandon it. But if we wish to see our denomination rise, and enlarge the sphere of its usefulness, let us come nobly to the work.

Our brethren at Granville have stood in the breach—they have resolved to risk all—and now when they look to us for aid, shall we desert them? It cannot be. Let our ministering brethren and others who feel a special interest in the cause of education among us, exert themselves, and something will be done. The time has come for *action*, and if we permit the present opportunity to pass away, we may never cease to regret it, nor our children to express their astonishment at our folly. To many the subject is new, to some uninteresting, and consequently *the few* will have to bear the burden and heat of the day—But let them decide promptly, give according as God has prospered them, and generations unborn will feel the influence of their instrumentality.

Lightning Source UK Ltd.
Milton Keynes UK
UKHW020021181218
334174UK00013B/2158/P